ELECTRICITY

by Meg Gaertner

Cody Koala

An Imprint of Pop!

popbooksonline.com

abdobooks.com
Published by Pop!, a division of ABDO, PO Box 398166, Minneapolis, Minnesota 55439. Copyright © 2020 by POP, LLC. International copyrights reserved in all countries. No part of this book may be reproduced in any form without written permission from the publisher. Pop!™ is a trademark and logo of POP, LLC.

Printed in the United States of America, North Mankato, Minnesota

052019
092019

Cover Photo: Shutterstock Images
Interior Photos: Shutterstock Images, 1, 11, 13, 14–15; iStockphoto, 5 (top), 5 (bottom left), 5 (bottom right), 7, 9, 17, 19, 21

Editor: Brienna Rossiter
Series Designer: Sarah Taplin

Library of Congress Control Number: 2018964773

Publisher's Cataloging-in-Publication Data

Names: Gaertner, Meg, author.
Title: Electricity / by Meg Gaertner.
Description: Minneapolis, Minnesota : Pop!, 2020 | Series: Science all around | Includes online resources and index.
Identifiers: ISBN 9781532163562 (lib. bdg.) | ISBN 9781532165009 (ebook)
Subjects: LCSH: Electricity--Juvenile literature. | Electric power--Juvenile literature. | Energy--Juvenile literature. | Science--Juvenile literature.
Classification: DDC 537--dc23

Hello! My name is
Cody Koala

Pop open this book and you'll find QR codes like this one, loaded with information, so you can learn even more!

Scan this code* and others like it while you read, or visit the website below to make this book pop.

popbooksonline.com/electricity

*Scanning QR codes requires a web-enabled smart device with a QR code reader app and a camera.

Table of Contents

What Is Electricity?

A boy flips a switch. Lights turn on. Next, he turns on the TV. Neither could work without electricity. Electricity is a form of **energy**. People use it in many ways.

Watch a video here!

Moving Electrons

Electricity is the **energy** of moving **electrons**. Electrons are tiny parts of **atoms**. Atoms join together to make many different materials.

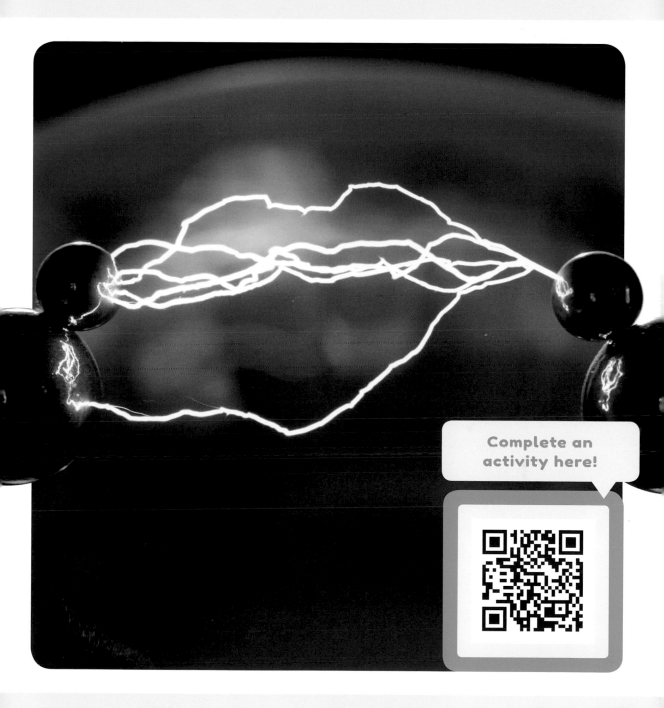

Complete an activity here!

In some materials, electrons can zip away from their atoms. These materials are called conductors. Electricity can move easily through conductors. Many kinds of metal are good conductors.

Metal power lines carry electricity to people's homes.

In other materials, electrons stay close to their atoms. These materials are called insulators. Electricity cannot move through them.

Wood, plastic, and glass are insulators.

Energy

Energy can take many forms. These include light, heat, and movement.

Learn more here!

Electricity can change
into other forms of energy.
It can light up a light bulb.

It can heat an oven. It can
turn a motor and make
a car move.

Circuits

Electricity can be stored in **batteries**. Batteries have two ends with opposite **charges**. One end is negative (−). The other end is positive (+).

Learn more here!

Electricity moves through **circuits**. Each circuit has a source of electricity, such as a battery. It also includes something to be powered by electricity. One example is a light bulb.

Two wires connect the light bulb to the battery. The wires carry **electrons** from the battery to the light bulb and back again. **Energy** from the moving electrons makes the light bulb glow.

Electrons have a negative charge. They move toward the positive charge.

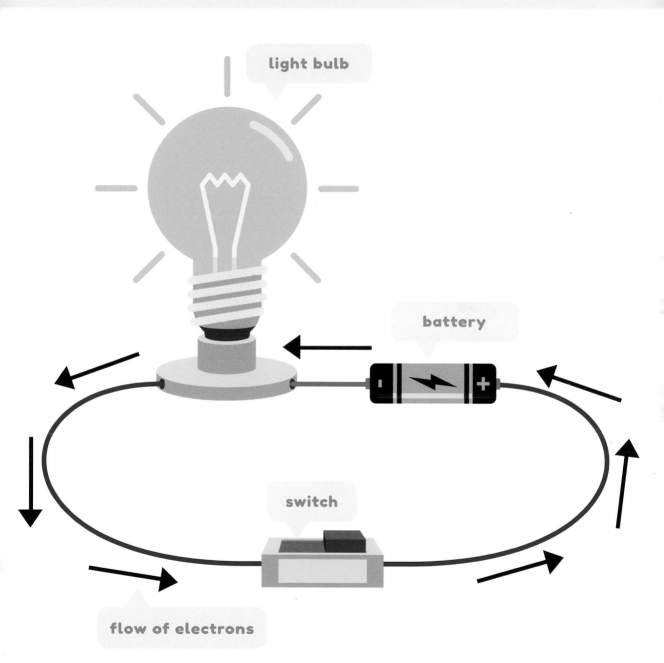

Making Connections

Text-to-Self

Have you used something that gets power from electricity? What was it?

Text-to-Text

Have you read other books about energy or electricity? What did you learn?

Text-to-World

How would life be different if people were not able to use electricity?

Glossary

atom – the smallest bit that matter can be broken into and still have the qualities of the original thing.

battery – a device that stores electricity and can be used to power certain items.

charge – the amount of electrical energy (either positive or negative) an object has.

circuit – a path for electrons to flow through.

electron – the part of an atom that has a negative charge.

energy – the ability to do work.

Index

Online Resources

popbooksonline.com

Thanks for reading this Cody Koala book!

Scan this code* and others like it in this book, or visit the website below to make this book pop!

popbooksonline.com/electricity

*Scanning QR codes requires a web-enabled smart device with a QR code reader app and a camera.